MUSICAL
INSTRUMENTS

# Pianos

Cynthia Amoroso,
Robert B. Noyed,
and John Willis

LET'S READ
AV²
BY WEIGL™
ADDED VALUE • AUDIO VISUAL

Go to **www.av2books.com**, and enter this book's unique code.

**BOOK CODE**

F852328

**AV² by Weigl** brings you media enhanced books that support active learning.

AV² provides enriched content that supplements and complements this book. Weigl's AV² books strive to create inspired learning and engage young minds in a total learning experience.

# Your AV² Media Enhanced books come alive with...

**Audio**
Listen to sections of the book read aloud.

**Key Words**
Study vocabulary, and complete a matching word activity.

**Video**
Watch informative video clips.

**Quizzes**
Test your knowledge.

**Embedded Weblinks**
Gain additional information for research.

**Slide Show**
View images and captions, and prepare a presentation.

**Try This!**
Complete activities and hands-on experiments.

# ... and much, much more!

Published by AV² by Weigl
350 5th Avenue, 59th Floor   New York, NY   10118
Website: www.av2books.com

Library of Congress Control Number: 2017936398

ISBN 978-1-4896-6010-7 (hardcover)
ISBN 978-1-4896-6011-4 (softcover)
ISBN 978-1-4896-6012-1 (multi-user eBook)

Printed in the United States of America in Brainerd, Minnesota
1 2 3 4 5 6 7 8 9 0  21 20 19 18 17

042017
310117

Project Coordinator: John Willis    Designer: Nick Newton

Weigl acknowledges Getty Images, Alamy, iStock, and Shutterstock as the primary image suppliers for this title.

MUSICAL
INSTRUMENTS

# Pianos

**In this book, you will learn about**

pianos

**what they are**

**how you play them**

**and much more!**

Watch her hands move quickly back and forth. She presses down on the keys. Plink, plink. Plunk, plunk. She is playing the piano!

The piano is a keyboard instrument. It has 88 keys. Some are black and some are white.

Most pianos have 52 white keys and 36 black keys.

The piano is also a string instrument. When a key is pressed, a hammer hits a string inside the piano.
The string vibrates.
The vibration makes a sound.

A piano is played with both hands. Fingers move up and down the keyboard to press the keys. Two parts of a song are played at once—one part with each hand.

Each key makes a different sound. The left keys sound low. The right keys sound high. A player touches a key softly to make a soft sound. A player pushes harder for a loud sound.

Piano players use their feet, too. They pump the pedals underneath the piano. Pedals change the piano's sounds.

Pianos have two or three pedals.

The first piano was made about 300 years ago in Italy. Now, pianos are played all over the world.

The first modern piano was invented by Bartolomeo Cristoferi in Florence, Italy.

Many schools and homes have pianos. Many children take piano lessons. They practice pressing the keys.

Some pianos are very large. Some are smaller. The piano makes many kinds of music. Two kinds of music are classical and jazz.

See what you have learned about pianos.

Which of these pictures does not show a piano?

# KEY WORDS

Research has shown that as much as 65 percent of all written material published in English is made up of 300 words. These 300 words cannot be taught using pictures or learned by sounding them out. They must be recognized by sight. This book contains 67 common sight words to help young readers improve their reading fluency and comprehension. This book also teaches young readers several important content words, such as proper nouns. These words are paired with pictures to aid in learning and improve understanding.

| Page | Sight Words First Appearance |
|------|------------------------------|
| 5 | and, back, down, hands, her, is, move, on, she, the, watch |
| 6 | a, are, has, have, it, most, some, white |
| 9 | also, makes, sound, when |
| 11 | at, both, each, of, once, one, parts, song, to, two, up, with |
| 12 | different, for, high, left, right |
| 15 | change, feet, or, their, they, three, too, use |
| 16 | about, all, by, first, in, made, now, over, was, world, years |
| 19 | children, homes, many, schools, take |
| 20 | kinds, large, very |

| Page | Content Words First Appearance |
|------|-------------------------------|
| 5 | keys, piano |
| 6 | instrument, keyboard |
| 9 | hammer, string, vibration |
| 11 | fingers |
| 15 | pedals |
| 16 | Bartolomeo Cristoferi, Florence, Italy |
| 19 | lessons |
| 20 | classical, jazz, music |